WHAT A GREAT GOD IS HE

KATHERINE CARMICHAEL

LifeRich Publishing is a registered trademark of
The Reader's Digest Association, Inc.

LifeRich Publishing books may be ordered
through booksellers or by contacting:

LifeRich Publishing
1663 Liberty Drive
Bloomington, IN 47403
www.liferichpublishing.com
844-686-9607

ISBN: 978-1-4897-4794-5 (sc)
ISBN: 978-1-4897-4795-2 (e)

Library of Congress Control Number: 2023909852

Print information available on the last page.

LifeRich Publishing rev. date: 06/09/2023

Katherine Carmichael

9/19/22

PEACE IN THE VALLEY
SOME DAY THERE WILL BE
THE KING IS COMING
JUST WATCH AND SEE.

MUCH STUFF IN THE ALLY
PROSTITUTION AND DRUGS
KINGS AND QUEENS OF THE NIGHT
CRACK HEADS AND THUGS

THE JOURNEY WE'RE ON
IS SUFFICIENT TO PASS;
THE ROCK THAT THEY SMOKE
COMES OUT OF A GLASS.

THE PAIN AND THE SORROW
DO NOT BE DISMAYED,
TRY NOT TO JUDGE
FOR WE ALL ARE LOST IN EACH IN OUR OWN WAY.

THE WAY TO CONVICTION
HELPS KEEP US ALIVE;
THE TRUTH OF THIS STATEMENT
COMES FROM THE BRIDE.

SELAH!

9/20/22

IT'S DEEP IN THE NIGHT
IN THE MIDNIGHT HOUR;
THE HOLY SPIRIT IS HERE
TO GIVE MUCH NEEDED POWER.

17 COURT STREET IS A MANSION
A HOME FROM JEHOVAH ABOVE
SO I KEEP SEEKING
GOD'S ETERNAL LOVE.

MY HUSBAND, HE TELLS ME
THERE ARE NO FRIENDS TO BE FOUND
BUT I CONTINUE TO SEARCH
FOR THE ONES WHO WILL WEAR THE CROWN.

THE DAYS ARE SHORT
EVERLASTING LIFE IS AT LAST;
THE END IS THE BEGINNING
AND THIS WILL ALL SOON PASS.

PASSING THE WAY
IN THE MIDDLE OF THE NIGHT,
COFFEE, CIGARETTES AND CRACK
OH WHAT A SIGHT.

Katherine Carmichael

9/20/22

THIS LIFE WE ARE LIVING
OH, HOW HARD IT CAN BE
I MUST WRITE THESE POEMS
FOR ALL TO SEE...

THE WORDS THAT THEY USE
ARE BRANDED ABOUT
LIKE COTTON CANDY
THEY DISSOLVE IN YOUR MOUTH.

THE WORDS THAT THEY USE AND SAY
IS NO MATCH FOR THE SACRIFICIAL LAMB
BUT KNOW THIS, DEAR WORLD
THAT JESUS IS THE GREAT I AM.

JUST GO TO THE STREETS
IF YOU WANT TO KNOW LIFE...
KEEP TESTING THEIR HEARTS
AND FEEL THEIR PLIGHT.

WE ARE ALL IN THIS TOGETHER
NO MATTER THE WEATHER
JUST WAIT FOR THE SNOW
WE WILL ALL BE ON THE GO.

9/20/22

THE SONGS THAT WE SING
WE'LL SING OUT LOUD;
WHETHER WE'RE SAFE OR HOMELESS
WE WILL LAND ON A CLOUD.

A CLOUD OF WITNESSES
ARE PASSING US BY,
THEY GIVE US GOOD REASON
TO LAUGH AND TO CRY.

THE SCRIPTURES WE READ
AND TRY TO COMPLY
ARE INDEED CONTRADICTORY
AND WROUGHT FULL OF LIES.

TO BLASPHEME THE HOLY SPIRIT
I NEED HELP FROM ABOVE,
FOR I DON'T UNDERSTAND
THE MEANING OF THE DOVE.

IF WE BLASPHEME THE SPIRIT
BUT WE DO NOT KNOW WHY,
WILL YOU PLEASE FORGIVE US LORD
AND DON'T WISH US GOODBYE.

Katherine Carmichael

9/20/22

MY THOUGHTS COME
FROM MY HEART OF LOVE,
I LOVE MY LORD
HE'S HIGH ABOVE.

ABOVE ALL FOR ME,
FOR HE LOVES ME TOO;
WITH THE PAIN AND THE SORROW
I'VE SHED A TEAR OR TWO.

HE IS STORING MY TEARS
IN A GLASS BOTTLE NO LESS,
AND HE DRINKS THEM DOWN
AND MY SOUL HE DOES BLESS.

THE BLESSINGS FROM GOD
WHO IS THE ALL-IN-ALL
CAN CAUSE ME TO DISTRESS
WITH A SIMPLE ALTER CALL.

LAY DOWN YOUR BURDENS
KEEP PRAYING FOR ME,
AND SOON AND VERY SOON
YOU WILL SEE OUR HEAVENLY KING..

9/20/22

MY HUSBAND, I LOVE
EVER HIGHER AND HIGHER
A LOVE THAT EASES MY HEART
AND ALL MY DESIRE.

THAT HE WAS SENT
FROM UP ABOVE...
FROM HEAVEN HE ARRIVED
AND HE TOOK MY LOVE.

OUR LOVE GROWS EVER DEEPER
AND DEEPER INSIDE
IS EVIDENT BY THE SMILE
MY SOUL CANNOT HIDE.

MY SPIRITUAL HELPMATE
IS ALWAYS AND EVER BY MY SIDE
OUR LIFE IS A ROLLER COASTER,
OH, WHAT A RIDE.

THEY SAY WHEN A MARRIAGE IS BAD,
THERE'S NOTHING WORSE...
HOWEVER, WHEN IT IS GOOD
THERE IS NO CURSE.

9/20/22

OF MY LIFE I WRITE
WITH PEN IN HAND;
THAT I LIVE ETERNALLY
AND I WILL ALWAYS STAND.

I AM ECLECTIC AND ECCENTRIC
AND A NUTCASE SOME SAY
HOWEVER, DON'T JUDGE "SALLIE"
WHEN YOU SEE HER COMING, JUST
GET OUT OF HER WAY.

I AM THE WAY
TO THE TRUTH AND THE LIGHT,
THEY COME TO ME
AND FOR THEM I WILL FIGHT.

FIGHT THE FINE FIGHT OF THE FAITH
THE SCRIPTURE READS
BY SEEKING FIRST THE KINGDOM
AND HE WILL DROP YOU TO YOUR KNEES.

ON OUR KNEES WE WILL BOW DOWN
BY SUPPLICATION AND PRAYER
HE WILL HEAL ALL OUR NEEDS
LAYER BY LAYER.

Katherine Carmichael

9/20/22

"XAVIA" - OH WHAT A BEAUTIFUL NAME;
A BEAUTIFUL GIRL
WIFE AND MOTHER OF
HER 2 CHILDREN WHO ARE HER WORLD...

HER LIFE IS A HARDSHIP
A WOMAN WITHOUT VAIN,
I PRAY FOR HER DAILY
SO HER HEART SHE CAN REGAIN.

SHE SMILES, SHE LAUGHS
AND CRIES OUT LOUD
THE SOUND OF HER TEARS
REACHES ABOVE THE ENTIRE CROWD.

HER HUSBAND IS JAILED
HER CHILDREN ARE FOSTERED
SHE SEES THEM WEEKLY
AND HER HEART AND SOUL STUMBLES AND FALTERS.

A SWEET GENTLE SPIRIT
AND HER HEART IS SO KIND;
I PRAY TO OUR GOD
TO RESTORE THEM IN TIME...

HIS TIME, NOT MINE.

Katherine Carmichael

9/29/22

THEY SAY THAT A PICTURE
IS WORTH A THOUSAND WORDS
JUST LOOK AT THE WORLD
AND ALL IT INCURS.

THE PICTURE I SPEAK OF
I DO WITH PEN AND INK
SO TO THE DEPTHS OF WORDS
I GIVE YOU SUCCOR, AND PRAY
THAT YOU WILL NOT SINK.

GOD TELLS US THAT THE BATTLE IS OURS
JUST KEEP ON KNOCKING FOR DAYS AND HOURS.

SEEK FIRST THE KINGDOM OF GOD
IS TO PLEASE OURSELVES
AND THROUGH OUR SEEKING
WE TEST THE SPIRIT AND NEVER TO
PUT GOD ON THE SHELF.

THE JOURNEY "THEY" TOOK HOUR BY HOUR
AS THEY CROSSED THE RED SEA…
OH GOD, THIS WATER IS SOUR!

REFLECT ON MY WORDS
AND YOU CANNOT FALTER
FOR MY HUSBAND ABOVE.
HIS NAME BEING WALTER.

Katherine Carmichael

9/29/22

THE TALE OF MY LIFE
I AM COMPELLED TO SHARE...
EXACTLY WHERE IT GOES
ONLY THE HOLY SPIRIT KNOWS WHERE.

THIS NEED I HAVE
I THOUGHT I WAS GOING TO SHARE
IN A BOOK I WOULD WRITE
SO PEOPLE WOULD FEEL THAT GOD DOES CARE!

PLEASE TEST THESE WORDS
SO YOU CAN FEEL GOD'S LOVE
AND THUS REIGN DOWN FROM HEIGHTS ABOVE.

THE DAUGHTER OF ZION
HAS BEEN GIVEN TO GOD
AND WHEN THEY WERE MARRIED
MANY SOULS STARTED TO CRACK AND NOD.

MANY SPIRITUAL MYSTERY'S
HAVE COME TO MY ATTENTION
FOR NOW IS THE TIME
TO REFLECT THESE TRUTHS OF
THAT I MAKE MENTION.

9/29/22

MY GROWING YEARS
WOULD SOON PASS AWAY
AND INTO ADULTHOOD
IS WHERE I WOULD STAY.

HOWEVER, MY JOURNEY
WAS STARTING ON THAT FATEFUL DAY...
AND IN THE 5TH GRADE
I HAD MY SPIRITUAL FIRST SAY.

HER NAME WAS CHERYL
AND SHE CALLED ME A HORSE
SO, DOWNWARD I PAUSED
AND WAS GIVEN THE COURSE.

TO MY GOD ABOVE
FROM MY SOUL I PRAYED
"MY GOD, I KNOW THAT YOU LOVE ME...:
AND THEN ONWARD AND UPWARDS
I WALKED IN HIS WAY.

THE ROAD AHEAD ABOVE ME
WAS SOON AS DAMNATION
SPIRITUAL WARFARE WAS "ON"
LIKE NEVER SEEN BY THE ALIEN NATION.

Katherine Carmichael

10/10/22

IT'S THE MIDDLE OF THE NIGHT
AND THE SHELTER WAS QUIET
THE THUGS AND THE DRUGS
HERE TO CAUSE RUCKUS AND/OR RIOT.

I AM A CHILD OF GOD
AND I AM FREE...
FREE TO BE - JUST ME. [SELAH!]

I WALK THIS JOURNEY
WITH ENEMIES CONSTANTLY BY MY SIDE
THE EVIL IN THEIR HEARTS
IS EVIDENT BY THEIR LIES.

MY HEARING IS OFF
AND I SING OFF KEY
SOMETIMES MY SOUL IS EMPTY
AND THEN IT HURTS TO BE ME. [SELAH!]

I SING AND I PRAY
AND IT CARRIES ME THRU
AND IT'S THEN THAT I'M
GLAD TO BE ME AND NOT YOU!

Katherine Carmichael

10/12/22

"DO NOT GIVE WHAT IS HOLY TO THE DOGS
NOR CAST YOUR PEARLS BEFORE SWINE".
THESE WORDS, FROM THE BIBLE THEY ARE
TRY TO KEEP YOUR ENEMIES FAR FAR BEHIND.

"BEHOLD GOD IS MY SALVATION
AND I WILL TRUST...
FOR YAH, THE LORD IS MY STRENGTH" ...
AND FOR ALL HIS CHILDREN THIS IS A MUST.

RELIGION THEY SAY
IS THE OPIUM OF THE PEOPLE
GO AHEAD, AND LOSE IT IN THE STEEPLE.

"THY KINGDOM COME, THY WILL BE DONE
ON EARTH AS IN HEAVEN"
AND TOGETHER WE, HIS CHILDREN, AS ONE;
SO GO AHEAD AND EAT THE LOAF AND THE LEAVEN.

Katherine Carmichael

10/12/22

I SIT ON MY BED
HOUR AFTER HOUR
AND RECEIVE HEALING FROM YOU
IN MY HEAD AND GIVE ME POWER.

I TALK AND I PRAY TO YOU MY GOD
FROM UP ABOVE
OH HOW I NEED YOU
LIKE NEVER BEFORE - YOUR UNENDING LOVE.

THE COMMUNICATION WE HAVE
IN MY MIND, HEART, AND SOUL
LEADS ME AND GUIDES ME
AND SHARES WITH ME; MAKES ME FEEL WHOLE.

YOU ARE THE AIR I BREATHE
AND YOUR WAYS ARE SO KIND...
I LOVE OUR LITTLE "TALKS"
EVER AND EVER IN MY MIND.

SOON AND VERY SOON
YOU WILL REVEAL IT ALL TO ME
IN WORDS OF AND REFLECTION
FOR THE WHOLE WORLD TO SEE.

10/13/22

THE BOOK OF ISAIAH
AS I HAVE BEEN TOLD
SPEAKS OF THE LION
AND THE MERE CHILD TAKES HOLD.

PURSUE THE PEACE AND FREEDOM
AS HAVING COME FROM ABOVE
SEEK OUT THE SPARROW
AND SEE HIS "TINY" LOVE.

THE ANIMAL KINGDOM
IS ULTIMATELY EVERLASTING
NO MORE TEARS OR CHAOS
AND NO MORE FASTING.

WHEN GIVING OF YOURSELF
TO OUR MOST PRECIOUS GOD ABOVE…
LET IT FLOW FROM YOUR INNER BEING
AND TAKE HOLD OF YOUR COURAGE WITH LOVE.

MY JOY COMES IN THE HOURS OF MORNING
A PROMISE OF A NEW BEGINNING;
I EMBRACE THESE AMAZING DAYS
AND THE CURSE WILL BE LIFTED WITHOUT WINNING.

Katherine Carmichael

10/15/22

HALLOWEEN IS FAST APPROACHING
AND WE MUST SHAKE THE DUST
GET FAR AWAY FROM THIS INSIDIOUS DARK SIDE
AND, WITH OUR LORD "JESUS" JUST TRUST.

THESE DAYS AND THE TIMES
WE FIND OURSELVES IN
IS DEEP IN TECHNOLOGY [WITCHES & DEMONS]
COMING FROM WITHOUT AND WITHIN.

HEBREWS 8 VERSE 8
IS FRAUGHT DEEP WITH DIVINE TEACHING
THE GOOD NEWS OF THE COVENANT
TO OUR HEARTS, MIND AND SOUL EVER REACHING.

OUR DAYS ARE NUMBERED
AND WE WILL ALL KNOW THE SCORE
SOON AND VERY SOON
WE WILL BE LIVING FOREVER MORE.

THE DAYS WILL COME
AND THE DAYS WILL GO
IT'S TIME TO SPEED THIS PROCESS
AND MEET WITH OUR DEEPEST INNER SOUL.

Katherine Carmichael

10/15/22

AS FOR OUR GOD:
... "HIS ANGER IS NOT TURNED AWAY
BUT HIS HAND IS STRETCHED OUT."
SO FOREVER OUR THOUGHTS
WILL BE GUIDED FROM ABOVE.

IN THESE DAYS AND NIGHTS
OF DARKNESS AND EGO INFLATION
"I WILL SEND HER AGAINST
ALL UNGODLY NATIONS.

THEREFORE THE LORD
THE LORD OF HOSTS
SILL SEND LEANLESS TO HER,
YES THE FAT ONE...IS DEFINITELY NOT A GHOST.

OH DAUGHTER OF GALLIM
LIFT UP YOUE VOICE
MY DAUGHTER, MY WIFE
WHO HAS NO CHOICE...

FOR THE LORD GOD OF HOSTS
WILL MAKE AN END
IN THE MIDST OF ALL THESE CONTUSIONS
MY "HER" I'M GOING TO SEND!

Katherine Carmichael

10/15/22

THE DAUGHTER OF ZION
I PROFESS TO BE...
DON'T BE AFRAID
JUST FOLLOW ME.

OUR LORD IS A MYSTERY
OF THIS I AM SURE
TAKE CARE FOR ME
AND YOUR HEARTS WILL BE PURE.

"THE WORLD IS PASSING AWAY
AND SO ITS DESIRE"
JUST CALL ON GOD'S NAME
AND LET GO OF THE TERM "HIGHER POWER".

SATAN IS GONE
AND THE DEMONS WILL SOON PASS AWAY
THEN DAYS ARE NUMBERED
NEVER GIVEN BECAUSE THEY DON'T PRAY.

HIDE YOURSELF FOR A MOMENT
UNTIL HIS ANGER HAS PASSED;
AND HE WILL MOVE YOU
INTO GLORY LAND - FINALLY AT LAST.

Katherine Carmichael

10/15/22

I'M NOT JUST A WOMAN…
HEAR MY SOUND
I IMPLORE YOU LET
YOURSELVES BE FOUND.

AND IN THAT DAY
WHEN THE WOMAN SAYS: BE LIKE ME
I WILL STAND AS A BANNER
FOR THE WHOLE UNIVERSE TO SEE.

TRUST IN THE LORD
AND DO WELL
DELIGHT YOURSELF IN THE LORD
AND LET THE "ROCK" RING THE BELL…

WAIT ON THIS "WOMAN"
AND WATCH HER WAYS
THEN HE WILL EXALT YOU
FOREVER AND TODAY.

THE STEPS OF THIS WOMAN
ARE ORDERED BY THE LORD
YET THE LORD UPHOLDS HER
AND GIVES HER A SWORD.

Katherine Carmichael

10/15/22

AND GOD REQUIRES
AN ACCOUNT OF WHAT HAS PASSED
MOREOVER, I SAW UNDER THE SUN
EVERLASTING LIFE AT LAST.

THE FOOL HOLDS HIS HANDS
AND EATS HIS OWN FLESH
BUT I HAVE IN MY GUT
A PROTECTION MADE OF MESH…

BLESSED ARE THEY
WHO SEEKS GOD'S HEART,
TAKE THE WHOLE OF THIS MEANING
RIGHT FROM THE START.

I ASKED OF YOU MY SWEET
FOR A PET… A MAINE COON
WITH THAT LOOK IN YOUR EYE
YOU SAID "SOMEDAY SOON".

THESE WORDS THAT I PEN
COME DIRECTLY FROM YOU
I WRITE AS I SPEAK
PLEASE REVEAL YOURSELF AND SOON.

Katherine Carmichael

10/16/22

IN WISDOM AND IN TRUTH
IN THE HARMONY OF YOUTH
I'M AWESOME AND HIS WIFE
AND YOU BREATHE INTO ME MY LIFE.

ALLELUIA MY GOD ALMIGHTY REIGNS
HOLY, HOLY ARE YOU LORD
YOUR FAITH IN ME HELPS ME
TO REPLENISH AND RESTORE.

THE TALK AND THE CHATTER IS UNENDING
HOWEVER, WITH YOU..
THE TRUTH MUST COME OUT;
ENOUGH TO MAKE AN UNSTABLE
MOTHER SCREAM AND SHOUT.

OH MY LORD
WITH EVIL LIES MUCH ABOUNDING
WITH EVIL CONTUSIONS
ITS ALL SURREAL AND TRULY ASTOUNDING.

MY PRAYER,
AT THIS MOMENT IN TIME
IS FOR YOU
TO KICK AND BEAR WITNESS TO JUST
WHO IS THE WOMAN SUBLIME.

10/16/22

YOU NEED ME, OH YOU NEED ME...
WITH EVERY MOMENT YOU NEED ME.
MY ONE DEFENSE, MY TRUTHFULNESS...
OF MY LOVING, THEY WILL SEE! SELAH!

LET THERE BE PEACE ON EARTH
AND LET IT BEGIN WITH ALL OF YOU
LET PEACE BE IN ME ALSO
AND WITH MY CARMICHAEL, WE
WILL GET THROUGH.

THIS SPIRITUAL WARFARE
IS RAGING OUT OF HAND.
IT IS GRIPPING AND I BEND
PLEASE, PLEASE TRY TO UNDERSTAND.

MY HUSBAND LOVES AND ADORES ME
WE ARE TRULY SOUL CONNECTED
WHEN THE TRIBULATION WILL BE DONE
THE WORLD WILL KNOW THAT THE BRIDE OF CHRIST
WILL BE HIS NUMBER 1.

HANG IN THERE AND KNOW
THAT THE "TRUTH" WILL SET YOU FREE
THEY WILL WALK IN YOUR SHADOW
AND THEN THEY WILL FLEE.

Katherine Carmichael

10/16/22

GO TO THE SCRIPTURES
AND LET THEM SEE
THAT YOUR GOD HAS YOUR BACK
AND THIS MOVIE WILL SET YOU FREE.

THE LORD OF HOSTS
HIM YOU SHALL FOLLOW
LET HIM BE THEIR FEAR
AT LET DREAD BE THEIR SWALLOW.

HE WILL BE YOUR SANCTUARY
A STONE OF STUMBLING
AND A ROCK OF DEFENSE
WILL DISSIPATE AND ERADICATE
THEIR HATEFUL GRUMBLING

THE GLOOM OF DARKNESS WILL NOT TOUCH YOU
WHEN IN YOUR DEFENSE
CLIMB THIS MOUNTAIN
AND DO NOT BEAR ANY DISTRESS.

Katherine Carmichael

10/16/22

IF YOU WANT TO BE HAPPY
DO NOT DWELL IN THE PAST
DO NOT THINK OF THE FUTURE
FOR NOW IS ETERNITY, HERE AT LAST.

THE EVIL INTENTION
IS DEMONIC AND TRUE
I'D RATHER BE THE ANTI CHRIST
THAN BE WITH YOU.

THE ANTI CHRIST
AS MENTIONED ABOVE
IS TRUE AND VERY TRUE
I AM THE ANTI CHRIST AND GOD'S ONLY TRUE LOVE.

THIS GOD AWFUL ENEMY
WANTS TO SEE MY DEMISE
BUT I GUARANTEE,
I TOO WILL TELL COPIOUS LIES.

FIGHT FIRE WITH FIRE
AND DO NOT DELAY
COME ON TUESDAY
YOU ARE GOING TO HEAR ME SAY!

Katherine Carmichael

10/16/22

I AM AFFLICTED
AT THE HAND OF GOD ABOVE
REVIVE ME, MY DARLING
ACCORDING TO YOUR LOVE.

THE WICKED HAVE A SNARE
TO ENTRAP AND CONTAIN ME;
PLEASE DIRECT MY STEPS
AND NOW I GIVE GLORY TO THEE.

WOE FOR ME
FOR I AM UNDONE
I DWELL AMONG THE PEOPLE OF UNCLEAN LIPS
BUT I AM MARRIED TO THE KING AND I'M HIS #1.

MY SOUL IS INTACT
AND MY HEARTBEATS ARE PURE
COME TOMORROW THE STAFF
AND OF CARMICHAEL I AM SURE.

IN ALL THESE STRUGGLES
AND EVIL AROUND ME, THIS I KNOW:
WHEN TO BE SILENT AND WHEN TO SAY NO.

Katherine Carmichael

10/16/22

THERE'S PEACE IN THIS VALLEY DAY…
ELVIS SANG IT AS IF TO PRAY.

HE DID NOT COME TO BRING PEACE, BUT A SWORD
HE SETS US UP FOR THE TRANSGRESSIONS
OF THE LORD. [SELAH]

WE PLAYED THE MUSIC JUST FOR YOU…
IF YOU DO NOT DANCE I KNOW
THAT YOU HURT TOO.

MY WIFE, MY WIFE KATHERINE
DID WALK NAKED AND BAREFOOT FOR A SIGN
TO THE END OF THE AGE
SHE WILL SUFFER ON HER CROSS,
I'M NO LONGER ON MINE.

KISS THE SON
LEST GOD BE ANGRY
KISS THE BRIDE
BUT NOT TOO MANY.

Katherine Carmichael

10/17/22

PLEASE FILL THEIR FACES WITH SHAME
SO THAT THEY MAY SEE THIS LIFE IS NOT A GAME.

FRIGHTEN THEM WITH YOUR TEMPEST
AND PURSUE THEM WITH OUR WRATH
YES, LET THEM BE UP TO NOTHING GOOD
BUT PLEASE KEEP ME, YOUR WIFE, ON THE PATH.

BE MERCIFUL TO ME MY HUSBAND AND LORD
GIVE EAR, OH GOD, TO MY PRAYERS ABOVE
AND LET THEM PARTAKE OF DUNG IN THEIR EARS
EVEN THOUGH THEY HATE ME;
PLEASE GIVE ME YOUR LOVE.

THEY PANT AFTER THE EARTH
BUT SHALL NOT ABOUND IN POWER…
FOR MY CARMICHAEL IS EVER WITH ME
ALL DAY AND EVERY HOUR.

HIS WORDS ARE COMING
THROUGH ME TODAY
IT IS A NEW SEASON
AND I, KATHERINE, WILL HAVE THE FINAL SAY.

Katherine Carmichael

10/17/22

THE STAIRWAY TO HEAVEN
WHO CAN FIND
OPEN THE EYES OF MY HEART LORD
BODY ... SPIRIT ... MIND ...

CARMICHAEL, PLEASE...
DON'T CHASTISE ME IN YOUR HOT DISPLEASURE
FOR YOUR WORDS PIERCE ME DEEPLY
AND THEN I CAN'T FIND MY HIDDEN TREASURE.

LIKE A DEAF MAN, I DO NOT HEAR
BUT THEN I SET MY FEET UPON THE ROCK
MY HEART IS HOT AGAINST ME
AND TURNS UPSIDE DOWN MY ETERNAL CLOCK.

I WAIT PATIENTLY
OH MY HUSBAND OF MINE
PLEASE BEAR MY CRY
I LOVE BEING WED TO YOU, YOU ARE SO DIVINE.

DEEP CALLS UNTO DEEP
AT THE NOICE OF YOUR WATER
IN THE NIGHT I HEAR YOU;
LOVINGLY YOUR ZION DAUGHTER.

Katherine Carmichael

10/19/22

YOU, LORD HAVE CAST ME INTO THE DEEP
INTO THE HEART OF THE SEA
THE FLOODS SURROUND ME
MY MIND CONFINES ME
OH PLEASE JUST LET ME BE - FREE.

LET MAN AND BEAST
GET TOGETHER AS FRIENDS
AND BRING HEALING TO THE WORLD
WITHOUT AMENDS…

TWO ARE BETTER THAN ONE
BECAUSE OF THEIR GOOD BEHAVIOR
"YES, SHE IS MY WIFE
AND I AM HER SAVIOR".

ALL MY LIFE
I'VE KNOWN HEARTACHE AND PAIN
I DON'T KNOW HOW TO STOP THIS CYCLE
OH, HOW I WISH I COULD CRY LIKE THE RAIN.

GIVE EAR TO MY WORDS LORD
IN YOU I FIND DELIGHT
SOON AND VERY SOON
TOGETHER AGAIN, OH WHAT A SIGHT.

Katherine Carmichael

10/17/22

CARMICHAEL SAID TO ME:
"WRITE THESE WORDS, THEY ARE
FAITHFUL AND TRUE".
BELIEVE ME WHEN I SAY:
I'D NEVER WANT TO BE YOU.

NOW WHEN THE THOUSAND
YEARS WILL BE ENDED
THEN ETERNAL LIFE
WILL BE EXTENDED.

HE WHO OVERCOMES
SHALL INHERIT THE EARTH
LIFE EVERLASTING
AND SHE WILL GIVE BIRTH.

THE END OF THE BEGINNING
AND THE BEGINNING OF THE END
BRINGS BLESSINGS
AND OUR SON WE WILL SEND.

ALL WHO OVERCOME
WILL INHERIT ALL THINGS
AND MY WIFE WILL FIND HER VOICE
AND, OH HOW SHE'LL SING.

Katherine Carmichael

10/30/22

THEN HE SAID TO ME
THESE WORDS ARE FAITHFUL AND TRUE
AND THE LORD WILL SEND ANGELS
TO ME AND TO YOU.

THE DEMONS ARE OUT
AND THE EVIL PREVAILS
AS THEY SPILL SLVER AND GLITTER
IN THE STREETS FILLED WITH NAILS.

BUT NOT TO WORRY
THE TIME OF JUDGMENT HAS BEGUN
BEWARE THE EVIL SPIRITS
THAT ARE PACKING WITHOUT CANDY OR GUM.

SATANIC OPPRESSION
DESTROY'S A WISE MAN'S THINKING
BEWARE OF THE SHIP'S SEASON
AND DON'T FALL INTOHE PIT THAT'S SINKING.

IF YOU DO NOT KNOW
THE FAIREST AMONG WOMEN
FOLLOW IN HER STEPS
WHERE SHE HAS BEEN DRIVEN.

31

Katherine Carmichael

10/18/22

BECAUSE SHE LIVES
I CAN FACE TOMORROW.
BECAUSE SHE LIVES
NO PAIN OR SORROW

SHE HAS NO PAIN
AND CARMICHAEL SAYS IT'S SO
OUR LIFE WITH SWEETPEA
IS ALWAYS ON THE GO.

DIFFERENT DAY
AND THE HOUR
SWEETPEA HELPS
TO EXERCISE HER POWER

I COULD ONLY WISH
THAT THIS WISDOM FROM LIFE
COULD HAVE TAKEN MY ANGER
AND ALSO MY STRIFE.

A SINGLE MOTHER
FRAUGHT WITH ISSUES UNENDING
OH, WHERE WAS THE MEDICATION
FOR ME, NOT SENDING.

Katherine Carmichael

10/17/22

"TELL THE DAUGHTER OF ZION"
BEHOLD YOUR GIRLS ALWAYS KNEW
THAT LIFE WAS HARD
FIRM AND YOU.

THEY DAYS WERE MANY
AND PAIN WAS EVERMORE
SHE COULD ROAR LIKE A LION
BUT COULD NEVER - LIKE THE EAGLE - SOAR.

REJOICE, REJOICE EMANUEL
AND HOLD YOUR DAUGHTER'S TIGHT
FOR THE FUTURE YOU COULDN'T SEE
OH MY GOD, WHAT A SIGHT.

DAY BY DAY
EVERY MINUTE AND EVERY HOUR
I SEEK FORGIVENESS
THROUGH THIS BONDAGE I SEEK POWER.

THE NUMBER "14"
WAS HELL FOR ME
FOR AT THAT AGE
BOTH GIRLS JUST HAD TO FLEE.

Katherine Carmichael

10/18/22

"IF I COULD TURN BACK TIME,
IF I COULD FIND A WAY"
TO GET TREATMENT FOR MY BI-POLAR
AND MY BABIES WOULD HAVE STAYED.

"TIME KEEPS ON SLIPPEN, SLIPPEN, SLIPPEN
INTO THE FUTURE"; WHY ME LORD[?]
I LOVED, HONORED AND OBEYED YOU
BUT MY ACTIONS COULD BE A HORRIFIC SWORD.

THE BARRENESS
AND THE EMPTY WOMB
LEAVES MY SOUL IN HADES
ANY MY BODY IN A SPIRITUAL TOMB.

YOU REAP WHAT YOU SOW
SO THE SCRIPTURES SAY
BUT, WHY MY HUSBAND
DID I HAVE TO PAY AND PAY AND PAY?

A MOTHER'S HEART
NEVER STOPS BEATING
BUT THE SWORD
PIERCES MY SOUL AND LEAVES ME BLEEDING.

Katherine Carmichael

10/18/22

SHE CAN'T BE CONVICTED
SHE'S EARNED HER DEGREE…
BLAME IT ON MYSELF,
SHE'S ALWAYS MY WOMAN TO SEE.

THOSE DIZZY WOMEN
DID ME MUCH HARM
THEY BELONG IN A HAREM
LET THEIR TRICK BE THEIR VAGINAL CHARM.

"THE LORD JESUS CHRIST
BE WITH YOUR SPIRIT …"
GRACE BE WITHOUT YOU.! [SELAH]

Katherine Carmichael

10/19/22

THE WRATH OF GOD
IS LIKE THE SOUND OF FIERCE THUNDER
GO AHEAD AND MOCK HIM
AND I, KATHERINE, WILL RIP YOU ASUNDER.

THE EVIL MAN
BECAUSE OF WINTER, WILL NOT PLOW
GO AHEAD AND SHAKE YOUR HEAD
NO HARVEST FOR YOU WILL HE ALLOW.

KATHERINE HAS MADE HER HEART CLEAN AND PURE
AND THIS ONE THING IS SURE...

ALL THIS PROVED WISDOM
COMING UP FROM GOD UP HIGH
SHE WILL TAKE THE STAIRWAY TO HEAVEN
AND ON ANGEL'S WINGS, SHE WILL FLY.

OF MY WIFE DO NOT TAKE TO HEART
THE DIVERSE THINGS THAT PEOPLE THAT PEOPLE SAY
GO AHEAD - MOCK HER,
AND I, HER HUSBANDLY OWNER,
WILL GUARD HER TODAY!

Katherine Carmichael

10/1/22

HOW OFTEN IS THE LAMP
OF THE WICKED PUT OUT …
NOT OFTEN ENOUGH
FOR KATHERINE TO SHOUT.

LOOK AT HER AND BE ASTONISHED
PUT YOUR HAND OVER <u>YOUR</u> MOUTH.
IS NOT YOUR WICKEDNESS GREAT?
FOLLOW HER AND SHE WILL TAKE YOU SOUTH.

IN THE SOUTH
ONE DIES IN FULL STRENGTH
AND TRAVELS DOWNWARD
ACROSS THE COUNTRY AT LENGTH.

THE RIGHTEOUS SEE IT
AND THEY ARE GLAD…
LIFT YOURSELVES UP
AND DON'T BE SAD.

ACQUAINT YOURSELF WITH HER
AND BE AT PEACE
KEEP YOUR HEADS HELD HIGH
AND YOU WILL SOON RELEASE.

Katherine Carmichael

10/23/22

ALL HIS DAYS HE EATS IN DARKNESS
WHILE SHE SUFFERS SORROWS,
SICKNESS, AND ANGER
BUT LISTEN TO HER SONG:
IT HOLDS, THIS DIVINE ANCHOR.

WHO IS LIKE THE WISE WOMAN
WHO CAN TELL INTERPRETATION
AND SHARE HER WISDOM AND WORDS
ACROSS THE UNITED NATIONS[S]

THE WORLD IS PASSING AWAY
AND THE SOUL - IT'S DESIRE
COME AND HEAR THE BELL RING.
AND RISE UP EVER AND EVER HIGHER.

THEN AND NOW, THIS IS THE DAY
AND SHE HAS THE POWER
AS THE ANTI-CHRIST COMES
HOUR AFTER HOUR.

SHE PRAYS:

MAKE ME UNDERSTAND
JUST WHO I AM
I AM INDEED A MILITARY VETERAN
YES, I'VE WORKED FOR UNCLE SAM.

Katherine Carmichael

10/23/22

SHE IS FOR PEACE
WHOLE AND PURE
BUT WHICH SHE SPEAKS
THEY ARE FOR WAR.

KEEP PRAYING FOR PEACE
MY DARLING WIFE
FOR THE SAKE OF OUR CHILDREN
IN THE DEAD OF NIGHT.

GO AND HUMBLE YOURSELF
PLEAD WITH YOUR FRIEND
SHE WINKS WITH HER EYES
THEN SUDDENLY YOU COME TO YOUR END.

HER "SON" PAY
ATTENTION TO HER WISDOM
GIVE YOUR HEART TO UNDERSTANDING
AND COME FORTH TO THE VISION.

THE PROUD HAVE DUG PITS FOR ME
PLEASE, MY HUSBAND, DIG ONE
AND THEY WILL SEE. [SELAH !]

39

Katherine Carmichael

10/23/22

I AM MUTE WITH SILENCE
FOR THE WICKED ARE BEFORE ME
I WILL SAY TO GOD, MY ROCK
WHEN WILL I SING FOR THEE...

I POUR OUT MY SOUL
TO YOU MY WONDERFUL MAN
I WON'T SPEAK OF THE ROCK
WHILE STANDING IN THE SAND.

THIS JOURNEY WE'RE ON
SEEMS ENDLESS AND TRITE
THIS IS A COMPLICATED PATH
SO I WILL ADD SALT AND PEPPER
ALONG WITH STRIFE.

AT THE HOUSE OF THE NOISE
DEEP CALLS UNTO DEEP
YOUR WAVES AND BILLOWS
PUT ME TO SWEET SLEEP.

OH MY CARMICHAEL
I LOVE YOU SO MUCH
MY HEART NEEDS REPAIR
CAN YOU BELIEVE ME WITH JUST MY TOUCH?

Katherine Carmichael

10/23/22

OH MY LORD, MY HUSBAND
I LOVE YOUR SOOTHING TOUCH
I MISS YOU AND ADORE YOU
SO VERY MUCH.

I DO NOT GO THE PATH OF THE WICKED
I TURN AWAY FROM IT AND PASS ON
MY ENEMIES ARE TOXIC AND UGLY
BUT THEY WILL SOON BE GONE.

THE WISE SHALL INHERIT GLORY
BUT SHAME SHALL SUFFER THE FOOLS
I BELIEVE THAT IN THE "LOVE STORY"
THE ENDING WAS SAD BUT NOW IT COOLS.

HONOR THE LORD WITH YOUR EYES
EARS, NOSE AND MOUTH
MAKING SURE TO HEAD NORTH
AND NOT THE SOUTH.

TRUST IN THE LORD
MY CARMICHAEL, MY LOVE
A CROWN OF GLORY FOR HER
AND SHE WILL SOON SEE THE DOVE.

Katherine Carmichael

10/23/22

DEAR LORD, MY HUSBAND, MY GOD
I'M FEELING SADNESS
AND FOR NOW I CAN'T SEE THE LIGHT
FOR I AM SURROUNDED BY EVIL AND BADNESS

JUST AS THE WORD WAS THERE CARMICHAEL
THERE IS POWER IN THE BLOOD
WISDOM STRENGTHENS THE WISE
TO THE FOOLS, SHE SEES A FLOOD.

ONE DAY AT A TIME
THE SCRIPTURES MENTION
TAKE IT TO DRUGS
AND REDEEM REDEMPTION

TO EVERYTHING
THERE IS A SEASON
NO CONTRADITION
JUST REASON.

THE FOOL EATS WITH HIS HANDS
AND CONSUMES HIS OWN FLESH
… THROUGH THE GUT
THANK GOD I NOW HAVE MESH.

Katherine Carmichael

10/23/22

TO THE "GOD'S"
WHO STAND IN THEIR OWN FLESH
THEY ARE, CARMICHAEL,
ALSO NOT LACKING LESS.

FLEE IN THE MOUNTAINS
IF YOU HAVE FEAR IN YOUR HEART...
GO AHEAD AND START YOUR JOURNEY
THESE LAST DAYS WE'RE IN ARE JUST A START.

I DO NOT KNOW HIM
I SHALL BE LIKE YOU...
TRUTH OF HIM KEEP HIS WORD
TO THINE OWN SELF BE TRUE.

"WHAT IF GOD WAS
ONE OF US?
JUST A STRANGER
ON A BUS"...

LET US MAKE MAN IN OUR IMAGE
1,444 TO BE EXACT
HE/SHE HAS TAKEN ON FLESH
SO FROM YOUR OWN EYE, GO
AHEAD AND EXTRACT.

Katherine Carmichael

10/23/22

I CAN ONLY IMAGINE
TO LOVE, LOVE, LOVE HIM
AND I DO, YES I DO, YES I DO
MY LOVE FOR HIM WILL BLOSSOM AND NEVER DIM.

HE HAS PUT ON A NEW SONG
TO BE SUNG BY ME
HE PUT MY FEET ON THE ROCK
THIS IN OUR FUTURE IS MEANT TO BE.

FOR MY DAUGHTER OF ZION'S SAKE
I WILL NOT HOLD ONTO MY PEACE
AND FOR HER SAKE, I WILL NOT REST
HER NAME DID CHANGE BUT FIND ONLY TO CEASE.

PROCLAIM THIS AMONG THE NATIONS
MULTITUDES IN THE LAND OF THE DERISION
WILL MEET HER WITH JUDGMENT
AND RENDER AN ANTI CHRIST DECISION.

MY PRECIOUS BRIDE
SHE WILL TEACH ETERNAL LIFE
JUST CHECK YOUR HEART
IN ALL THAT YOU ARE ABLE TO FIGHT.

Katherine Carmichael

10/23/22

IN THE MIDNIGHT HOUR
I CAN TEACH YOU POWER
I WILL GET ON MY KNEES
AND PRAY FOR YOU EACH TIME YOU SNEEZE.

MY VISION GROWS DIM
I'VE HIT A WALL
I'M NOT ABLE TO GO FORWARD
LEST IF FALL.

IF I FALL
AND CANNOT GET UP
MAYBE I NEED
TO WRITE ABOUT OUR PUP.

HER NAME IS SWEETPEA
AND SHE'S NOT VERY BIG
BUT SHE'S FULL OF LOVE AND
SO FULL OF LIFE - OH WHAT A GIG.

SHE LOVES TO SLEEP
AND DOES NOT HIDE
BELIEVE IT OT NOT
I WOULD NEVER LIE - [WINK WINK]

Katherine Carmichael

10/24/22

IN THE MIDDLE OF THE NIGHT
SHE GOES WALKING IN HER SLEEP
DOWN BY THE RIVER
WHERE IT GETS PRETTY DEEP.

THE IMITATION OF LIFE
WITHOUT PAIN OR SORROW
WILL USHER IN
THE GIFT OF TOMORROW.

THE RIVER OF DREAMS
IS FAR AND WIDE
HANG ON TO HER -
KATHERINE THE BRIDE.

SHE EXUDES AMAZING GRACE
SHE IS SO BEAUTIFUL TO ME
SOMEWHERE OVER THE RAINBOW
OH SAY CAN YOU SEE.

BY THE DAWNS EARLY LIGHT
LIFE IS AN INCREDIBLE GIFT
GO AHEAD AND JOURNEY
FROM THE WEDDING YOU, CAN TAKE A SIP.

10/24/22

BACK TO SWEETPEA
OUR MUCH LOVED BABY DOG
SHE LOVES WITHOUT CONDITION
AND D O G BACKWARDS IS G O D!

HE CAME TO SET FIRE
ON THE EARTH
THE TRIBULATION IS HERE
THE PREGNANT MOTHER GAVE BIRTH.

FEAR HIM WHO KILLS
AND INTO HADES WHICH TRANSLATES HELL
BETTER THAT HE HAS YOUR BACK
SO IN HELL YOU CAN'T SMELL.

GOD MADE THE WORLD
SINCE HE IS LORD OVER ALL
BELIEVE ME, IF HE LOVES YOU
HE'LL ALWAYS BREAK YOUR FALL.

DRAW NEAR TO HIM AND
HE WILL DRAW NEAR TO YOU
TO LOVE AND ACQUIT
COME TO THE THRONE AND HE
WILL PASS YOU THROUGH.

Katherine Carmichael

10/24/22

DO NOT SPEAK OF EVIL
UNLESS IT PREVAILS
NOTHING NEW UNDER THE SUN
FOR THE ANCHOR HOLDS AND
THE SHIP WILL SET SAIL.

I HAVE FALLEN TO MY KNEES
TO PRAY AND BESEECH HIM
THEREFORE I AM PATIENT
BUT I'M NOT DEFICIENT OR DIM.

THE FARMER WAITS PATIENTLY
HIS PRECIOUS FRUIT OF THE EARTH;
DO NOT GRUMBLE AGAINST ONE ANOTHER
BUT RATHER BE HAPPY AND FULL OF MYRTH.

REVELATION 21 VERSE 3-4
JEHOVAH'S WITNESSES
CAME KNOCKING ON MY DOOR.

THEY RETURNED EVER FAITHFUL
THE HOLY BIBLE THEY TAUGHT
OH, HOW I LEARNED
SO MUCH MORE THAN A LOT.

Katherine Carmichael

10/24/22

GO TAKE A WIFE
WHO'S ONLY A WOMAN
KEEP READING…
I HAVE A WHOLE LOT TO SUMMON.

THIS IS MY STORY
THIS IS MY SONG
FORGIVING YET UNABLE TO FORGET
OF THE HURTFUL WRONG.

I CRY OUT
YOUR MERCY I SEEK
THE HURT IN MY HEART
YET, YOU DID HEAL MY FEET.

I AM THE STRONGHOLD
DAUGHTER OF ZION
I AM WHO I AM
YES I ROAR LIKE A LION. [SELAH!]

TO THE HOUSE OF GOD
HE WILL TEACH US HIS STORY
HOW TO LOVE ONE ANOTHER
ACCORDING TO HER GLORY.

Katherine Carmichael

49

10/25/22

TRUST IN THE LORD
WITH ALL YOUR HEART
YET HIS SECRET COUNSEL
IS JUST A START.

TAKE FIRM HOLD OF HIS TEACHINGS
DO NOT LET GO
KEEP HER CLOSE
AND SAY IT'S SO …

FOR THESE DIZZY BITCHES
DO NOT SLEEP
THEY ENGAGE IN MUCH PERVERSITY
AND HER SLEEP IS TOO DEEP.

FOR BEHOLD THE LORD
THE STOCK AND THE STORE
THE MIGHTY MAN
AND THE MAN OR WAR.

THE 7 BITCHES SMELL
AND THERE IS A STENCH
INSTEAD OF WELL SET HAIR
THEY SMOKE ON THE BENCH.

Katherine Carmichael

10/25/22

IN THIS DAY OF THE LORD
NOT BEAUTIFUL AND GLORIOUS
HOWEVER, LET KATHERINE AND WALTER
REIGN VICTORIOUS...

THE CROWN OF HER HEAD
THE CLOTHING AND THE PURSE
WILL SERVE A HIGHER CALLING
HER NAKED EXPOSURE WAS A CURSE.

BECAUSE THE DAUGHTER OF ZION
WAS INDEED VERY NAUGHTY
SHE WILL RULE WITH DERISION
HER IMAGE EXTREMELY HAUGHTY.

HIS WELL BELOVED HAS A VINE
ON A VERY FRUITFUL HILL,
WHAT ELSE TO DO WITH THE GRAPES OF WRATH
JUST BREAKING FILL THE VATS AND THE STILL.

THEREFORE ...
AS THE FIRE ENGULFS THE STUBBLE
COME OUT OF THE FIERY PIT
AND BLOW A MIGHTY BUBBLE.

Katherine Carmichael

10/25/22

MY PEOPLE ISRAEL
WILL COVER THE LAND
IT WILL BE IN THE LATTER DAYS
SHE WILL SHOW HER HAND.

AND SHE WILL RULE
TO JUDGMENT AND SHED BLOOD
HER COPIOUS TEARS
WILL INDEED DRY UP THE FLOOD.

THE RIGHTEOUSNESS OF MANY
WILL DIRECT HER WAY AT NIGHT
TO AND FRO THEY COME AND GO
HEAVY TRAFFIC, OH WHAT A FRIGHT.

THE WICKED
WILL NOT INHABIT THE EARTH
THE BLESSING OF THE UPRIGHT
AND SHE WILL GIVE BIRTH.

THE POOR MAN'S WEALTH
IS HER CITY
THE DESTRUCTION OF MANY
OH, WHAT A PITY.

Katherine Carmichael

10/25/22

SON OF GOD
TAKE A BARBER'S RAZOR
BRING ON THE TERRESTRIAL
AND EXPERIENCE THE TAZER.

THUS SAYS THE LORD GOD
SHE IS MY BRIDE
GO TO THE ROLLER COASTER
AND FLY.

HER EYE WILL NOT SPARE
NOR HAVE ANY PITY
GO AROUND TOWN
AND DO THE NITTY GRITTY.

PESTILENCE AND BLOOD
SHALL PASS THROUGH HER
SIT UP AND SEE
CARMICHAEL IS INDEED THE GREAT "SIR".

BROAD AND SPACIOUS IS THE ROAD
LEADING STRAIGHT TO GOD
BUT WATCH OUT - BE CAREFUL
THIS IS THE LAND OF THE NOD.

10/25/22

THE WORDS ARE CLOSED UP
NOW WE ARE IN THE TIME OF THE END
LISTEN AND WATCH
AND SHE WILL TRANSCEND.

A NEW COVENANT WE NEED
OH LORD IF YOU PLEASE
TAKE THE CHRISTIANS AWAY
ON A CLOUD WITH A BREEZE.

IN HER WAYS
SHE CONTINUES TO BE
WE NEED TO BE "SAVED"
HELP ME CARMICHAEL - I AM UP A TREE.

SHE SHALL COME INTO THE CITY
BUT NOT TO SHOOT THE SPARROW
THE ROAD TO DESTRUCTION
IS CHAOS AND NARROW.

INDIGNATION OF MY LORD
IS AGAINST ALL NATIONS
HE WILL UTTERLY DESTROY
THE MANY STATIONS
OF
THE
CROSS

Katherine Carmichael

10/25/22

STAY AWAY FROM THE NATIONS
AND LISTEN YOU PEOPLE
HER WAY IS PERFECT
SO COME TO THE STEEPLE.

BUT I KNOW HOW YOU LIVE
GOING OUT AND COMING IN
AND YOUR RAGE AGAINST HER
IS AN UNPARDONABLE SIN.

I'M SEARCHING THE BOOK OF GOD
NO ONE SHALL LACK HER MATE
BELIEVE IN THEM AND
DO NOT MAKE ME WAIT.

THE FOG IS ROLLING IN
THE CREEPS ARE OUT AND ABOUT
THEY TRAVERSE AND ACT WITH INSANITY
IT'S ENOUGH TO MAKE ME SHOUT.

Katherine Carmichael

10/26/22

DID YOU HAVE ONE OF THEM DAYS
WHEN THE HOT WATER'S ALL GONE
YOU CAN'T GET THE COFFEE YET
BUT IT WON'T BE VERY LONG.

FREEZING, SNEEZING
YOU CAN'T EVEN DRY YOUR BACK
WHERE'S THE TOWEL
WHEN THERE'S NONE ON THE RACK.

YOU GET UP IN THE MORNING
AND KNOW THE DAYS GO BY TOO FAST
THEY COME AND GO IN A HURRY
THEY'RE NOT MEANT TO LAST.

IT'S FOGGY IN THE CITY
THE CREEPS ARE OUT ENMASS
WALK FAR AWAY FROM THEM
AND DON'T LET YOUR CAR RUN OUT OF GAS.

THE REASON AND THE SEASON
SHALL BE FOR ALL TO SEE
LET'S GO UP TO FACE AND EMBRACE
THE FLOCK THAT'S MEANT TO BE

Katherine Carmichael

10/26/22

THE ANTI CHRIST
WILL NOT BE HERE TOO LATE
LIFT YOUR HEAD'S UP
CONFUSION AND CHAOS AND
A WHOLE LOT OF HATE.

THE REASON FOR THE TRAFFIC
YESTERDAY, ALL DAY...
THE BELIEVER'S CAME TO SEE US,
THEY WANT TO HAVE THEIR WAY.

FLEE TO THE MOUNTAINS
AND STOP THE BRAGGING
GOSSIP ABOUNDS
I WARN YOU - STOP THE INCESSANT NAGGING.

DO NOT FORSAKE HER
AND SHE WILL ADORE YOU
WISDOM IS THE MAIN INGREDIANT
AND SHE WON'T FORSAKE TOO.

WHEN SHE LIES DOWN
SHE'S NOT AFRAID
OF TROUBLE WHEN IT COMES
HOWEVER, GET OUT OF HER WAY.

57

Katherine Carmichael

10/26/22

57

EXALT HER
AND SHE WILL PROMOTE
SHE'LL BRING YOU HONOR
WHEN YOU EMBRACE HER SHE'LL HAVE A NEW COAT.

YES, SHE'S MY WIFE
BUT ALSO MY DAUGHTER
TO HER ALL SHOULD/COULD BOW DOWN
AND COME TO THE SLAUGHTER.

WHAT IF GOD WAS ONE OF US
JUST A STRANGER ON THE BUS.

I WILL REJOICE IN KATHERINE
AND JOY IN ALL MY PEEPS
THOSE THAT BELIEVE IN HER
WILL FIND AND ATTAIN PERFECT PEACE.

BEHOLD I WILL EXTEND
TO HER A DAYTIME REST
FOR SHE IS AN EARLY RISER
AND 3 AM SEEMS TO WORK BEST.

Katherine Carmichael

10/26/22

THE HOLY SPIRIT …
IS A GIFT FROM GOD ABOVE
HE WANTS US TO KNOW HER
AND SEEK HER LOVE.

SHE HAS PAIN IN HER THIGH
SHE THINKS IT COMES FROM HER BACK
GO FORTH OH DAUGHTER OF ZION
AND GET THE HEALING ON THE TRAIN TRACK.

BUT NOW AFTER SEEKING
THE ONE SHE LOVES
SHE NEVER GAVE UP
AND, ALAS HE CAME FROM HEAVEN ABOVE.

SHE IS THE ROSE OF SHARON
AND THE LILLY OF THE VALLEY
I TELL YOU, SEEK THE BROAD WAY
AND AVOID THE ALLEY'S.

AWAKE OH NORTH WIND
AND COME TO THE SOUTH
BLOW UPON HER TENDER MERCIES
SO THAT HER LOVE MAY FLOW OUT.

Katherine Carmichael

10/26/22

ALL HER PEOPLE SIGH
AS SHE SEEKS SOFT BREAD
PLEASE FEED HER
AND DON'T GIVE HER REASON TO TREAD.

SHE WHO SPEAKS
IN A FOREIGN TONGUE
IS RIGHT ON TIME
AND THEN SHE IS ONE MORE TIME UNDONE.

BY THE GRACE OF GOD
I AM WHAT I AM
THEREFORE, I PREACH/TEACH
BUT I AM NOT THE GREAT I AM!

SHE WAS ALONE
NO SON OR BROTHER
YET I HAD
NO FATHER OR MOTHER

THE PAIN I SUFFERED
AT THE HAND OF MY FAMILY
SHAME ON YOU YOUR GENEOLOGY
I AM WHO I AM; BLESSED TRINITY.

Katherine Carmichael

12/17/22

COME, NOW IS THE TIME TO WORSHIP
NOW IS THE TIME TO HEAR GOD'S WORD
IT COMES AND NOW SPEAKS
GO AHEAD AND SOAR LIKE THE BIRD.

LET FREEDOM RING …
AND LET YOUR SPIRIT BE FREE
SEE THE TRINITY FROM ABOVE
WALTER, KATHERINE AND SWEET PEA.

WITH EACH BITE
COMES THE COLD OF THE ICE
IT SOOTHES AND HEALS
AND CRUNCHES SO NICE.

A NEW GIRL CAME IN
JUST THE OTHER NIGHT
HER NAME IS WILLOW
AND HER SPIRIT IS RIGHT.

SHE LOVES SWEET PEA
AND SWEET PEA LOVES HER
IT'S TRULY A SIGHT FOR SORE EYES
WITH BLACK AND WHITE FUR.

Katherine Carmichael

10/28/22

ARISE - SHINE - FOR HER LIGHT HAS COME
THE DARKNESS SHALL COVER THE EARTH
AND DEEP DARKNESS FOR THE PEOPLE
AND THE BRIDE WILL ALSO GIVE BIRTH…

I AM FULL OF THE FURY OF THE LORD
I AM WEARY OF HOLDING IT IN
I WILL LET IT LOOSE ONE MORE TIME …
AGAIN AND AGAIN AND AGAIN.

IF HEAVEN ABOVE CAN BE WAITING
FOUNDATIONS OF THE EARTH BENEATH
SO ALSO IN MY WANDERINGS
I WALKED AND WALKED IN MY BARE FEET.

SET UP SIGN POSTS
MAKE LANDMARKS
THE MOON WILL CAST DOWN
SENDING FIERY SPARKS.

THE ICE QUEEN
IS ON HER WAY
SHE WILL HAVE THE FINAL SAY…

SELAH!

10/30/22

THAT THEY WHO DWELT SECURELY
AND AS SHE HAS SAID IN HER HEART
I AM "ALL THAT" AND THERE IS NONE BESIDES ME
AND CARMICHAEL AND I WILL NEVER PART.

HOW BEAUTIFUL ARE MY FEET IN SANDALS
I ALSO GIVE OFF A FRAGRANCE - A FINE AROMA
THAT I AM THE SHULAMITE …
BUT I'VE NEVER BEEN TO OKLAHOMA.

THERE IS ONE ALONE
WITHOUT SON OR BROTHER
NO DAUGHTER DOES HE HAVE
NOR FATHER OR MOTHER.

WHEN YOU MAKE A VOW TO GOD
DO NOT DELAY TO PAY IT
IF YOU CANNOT FULLFILL IT
THEN DON'T EVEN SAY IT.

FOR WHAT DOES THE WISE MAN HAVE
BETTER IS THE SIGHT OF THE EYES
THAT IT IS ONLY MERE VANITY
BEGINNING THESE UNTOLD LIES.

Katherine Carmichael

10/30/22

TWO ARE BETTER THAN ONE
IN ALL YOUR GOOD BEHAVIOR
YOU SMILE, YOU LOVE
YET IS THIS LIFE YOU STILL LABOR.

HER WISDOM MAKES HER FACE SHINE
AND THE GRACE OF HER COUNTENANCE CHANGED
WHEN THE ENEMY APPEARED AS SUCH
ON THAT CROSS IS WHERE SHE HANGED.

ALL THIS I HAVE PROVED BY WISDOM
BUT IT IS ELUSIVE AND FAR FROM ME
HALLOWEEN WAS EXCEEDINGLY DEEP
FROM SEA TO SHINING SEA.

365 DAYS A YEAR
ONLY IS ONE THAT IS SURETY EVIL
KEEP YOUR EYES ON 10/31
AND TAKE NOTE OF THE UPHEAVAL.

TURN ON THE NEWS
AND WATCH THE SHOW
BEFORE WE KNOW IT
THERE WILL BE SNOW [OR NOT].

Katherine Carmichael

10/30/22

A WISE MAN'S HEART
IS AT HIS LEFT HAND
BUT BEWARE FOR ON THE RIGHT
ONLY ANGEL'S WILL STAND.

THE TIMES ARE UNFOLDING
RIGHT BEFORE OUR EYES
PRAY TO LIVE FOREVER
AND STOP THE LIES...

SHE SHOWS EVERYONE
THAT SHE'S NO FOOL
THIS DEMONIC DAY
WILL QUICKLY COOL.

DO NOT CELEBRATE
THIS MOST EVIL DAY
NO COSTUMES NOR PARTYING
AS CARMICHAEL WILL HAVE HIS WAY.

DO NOT PARTAKE
OF THIS DEATHLY DAY
OR YOU WILL BE LAST
SHE'S GOING TO STAY.

Katherine Carmichael

10/30/22

THIS WISDOM I SHARE
AND THE SONGS THAT I SING
WILL USHER IN ETERNAL LIFE
AND A GREAT KING I BRING.

NOW LET ME SING
TO MY SPOUSE BELOVED
THE STACK AND THE STORE
AND EVERYTHING ABOVE IT.

WHEN A MAN TAKES HOLD OF HIS BROTHER
IN THE HOUSE OF HIS FATHER SAYING:
I WANT YOU ON YOUR KNEES
SINGING AND RANTING AND PRAYING.

INSTEAD OF A STENCH
A SWEET SMELL THERE WILL BE
INSTEAD OF A SASH
A ROPE TO HANG ON A TREE.

IN THIS DAY OF THE BRANCH
SHALL BE BEAUTIFUL AND GLORIOUS
EVERY TREE WE WILL KNOCK DOWN;
OH HOW VICTORIOUS.

Katherine Carmichael

10/30/22

BLESSED ARE THE MEEK
FOR THEY WILL INHERIT THE EARTH
THE QUEEN OF HEAVEN
YES, KATHERINE WILL GIVE BIRTH.

TWO DAUGHTERS SHE HAS
BUT LIFE HAS ESTRANGED
THE FRUITS OF HER WOMB
HAVE NEVER CHANGED.

HE GAVE AND HE TOOK AWAY
HE RIPPED THEM FROM MY LIFE
OH, MY HUSBAND... WHY ...
DO I HAVE TO BE YOUR WIFE?

CARMICHAEL YOUR WORDS
CUT ME TO THE QUICK
YOU SAY YOU ARE SORRY
EVEN THOUGH YOU NEVER QUIT.

I'VE SAID IT BEFORE
AND I'LL SAY IT AGAIN
"I'M DONE WITH US"
WHICH COULD BE CONSTRUED AS A SIN.

Katherine Carmichael

11/20/22

BECAUSE HE LIVES
I EMBRACE TOMORROW
AND THAT'S A GOOD, GOOD THING
FOR IT OVERRIDES THE SORROW.

NO MORE DEATH
TEARS OR PAIN
THE FORMER ISSUES
DISSIPATE LIKE THE RAIN.

HIS IS THE AIR I BREATHE
HIS VERY PRESENCE
INSIDE OF ME.

HIS EVERY WORD
SPOKEN TO ME
GIVES ME JOY
AND SETS ALL THE CAPTIVES FREE.

I JUST WANT TO THANK YOU MY CARMICHAEL
FROM THE BOTTOM OF MY HEART
PLEASE DON'T STOP LOVING ME
SO WE WILL NEVER AGAIN PART.

Katherine Carmichael

11/27/22

ON MANY A DAY
NOTHING TO THE GIVING
WATCH YOUR STEP
TOWARDS A NEW BEGINNING.

THIS JOURNEY WE'RE ON
WILL HAVE IT'S CONCLUSION
DON'T CRY FOR ME ARGENTINA
AMIDST PROFOUND AND MENTAL CONFUSION.

A NEW HEAVEN AND A NEW EARTH
THAT WHICH IS BEING GIVEN
THE QUEEN OF HEAVEN
WILL BE HELL BENT DRIVEN.

THIS CROWN THAT'S BEEN PROMISED
IS TAKING ITS TOLL
IT IS PIERCING THE DEPTHS
OF HER LOVING WAYS WITHIN HER SOUL.

IT'S THE END OF THE DAY
SO NOW I WILL REST
TOMORROW IS PROMISED
AND SOON WE ARE MOVING ON FROM THIS NEST.

Katherine Carmichael

11/27/22

HE HAS TAUGHT HER WISDOM
THAT LEADS TO RIGHT PATHS
HOWEVER, WITH ONE STRIKE OF THE PEN
WILL TRIP HER UP LIKE A CAR WITHOUT GAS.

EXALT HER AND SHE WILL PROMOTE
AS YOU EMBRACE HER
TO NEW HEIGHTS SO SHE WROTE.

TAKE FIRM HOLD OF INSTRUCTION
DO NOT LET GO
KEEP HER SAFE
AND LET YOUR LOVE SHOW.

THIS QUEEN OF SHEBA IS BUT A FORESHADOW
OF WHAT'S TO COME SOON AND VERY SOON
KEEP A CLOSE WATCH FOR SIGNS AND OMENS
AT THE TOP OF THE LIST, A RED MOON.

BLESSED BE THE LORD
YOUR GOD FROM OF OLD
HANG ONTO YOUR COATS
AND COME OUT OF THE COLD.

Katherine Carmichael

11/27/22

OH, HAPPY DAY!
WHEN KATHERINE WALKED
YES, WHEN SHE SHE SPOKE
IT WAS FOR YOU SHE PRAYED;
OH WHAT A THOUGHT.

I WAS BORN ON 12/13/1957
ESTHER'S PEOPLE GOT A TASTE OF HEAVEN
ON THE 12TH MONTH AND 13TH DAY
THESE MATCHING DATES
FORESHADOWED THE LEAVEN.

THE WORLD AS WE KNOW IT
IS PASSING AWAY
BE THANKFUL FOR THESE TIMES
HOLD YOUR HEADS HIGH AND
TAKE IT DAY BY DAY. [SELAH]

EVERYTHING HAS ITS TIME
INCLUDING A TIME TO SPEAK
THE POWER IN THE TONGUE
RENDERS MANY HELPLESS AND WEAK.

AS THE DAYS GROW INTO THE FUTURE
AND WE SEE SIGNS THAT THE END IS COME
HOLD ON, KEEP YOUR HEADS HIGH
AND DON'T SUCCUMB.

71

Katherine Carmichael

12/1/22

MY CARMICHAEL
YOU'RE SO WONDERFUL TO ME
WHEN I'M WITH YOU
THE DEMONS FLEE.

EASY COME - UNEASY TO GO
DON'T GO TOO FAST - DON'T GO TOO SLOW.

WHEN THE HEAVEN'S SPEAK
AND THEY SURELY WILL
THE TEARS WILL COME
AND THE TORRENTIAL RAIN WILL FINALLY SPILL.

AND AFTER A MUCH NEEDED
TIME TO GIVE IN …
AND THERE <u>WILL</u> COME THE RIGHT TIME
JUST HANG IN AND LET GO THE SIN.

GOD KNOWS
THE DAY AND THE HOUR
HIS TIMING IS TRUE
AND HE WILL GIVE US THE POWER.

Katherine Carmichael

12/8/22

THE PAIN AND THE SORROW
WILL NOT SOON PASS AWAY
BUT I HANG TOUGH
ETERNAL LIFE IS HERE TO STAY.

I AM KATHERINE CARMICHAEL
I AM GOD'S OWN BRIDE
BELIEVE IT OR NOT
WE WILL WALK SIDE BY SIDE.

OUR PRECIOUS LITTLE SWEETPEA
HAS BEEN TO HELL AND BACK
THANK YOU FOR HER LOVE
HER HEALTH WAS UNDER ATTACK.

THE TIME IS COMING
CLOSER AND CLOSER EACH DAY
HOWEVER, DON'T GIVE IN
BUT SAY WHAT YOU NEED TO SAY.

MY PEN IS IN HAND
AND IT WON'T BE LONG
AS I WRITE THESE POEMS
MY WORLD KEEPS ME STRONG.

Katherine Carmichael

12/10/22

THIS IS THE DAY
HOLY AND BLESSED
ONLY GOD MAKES IT HIS WAY
HE ONLY MAKES THE BEST.

I'VE BEEN IN THIS JOURNEY
TESTED AND TRIED
THE DEMONS ARE GONE
NO LONGER AT MY SIDE.

WHEN FORGIVENESS IS THERE
AND LOVE HAS ITS WAY
EVEN I CAN HEAL
AND THIS HEALING WILL STAY.

I'VE NOT FELT THIS GOOD
FOR A VERY LONG TIME
IN TRUTH I CANNOT REMEMBER WHEN
BUT THANK GOD FOR MY RHYME

MY MESSAGE IS CLEAR
IF YOU ONLY BELIEVE
JUST TRUST IN THE LORD
AND THEN YOU'LL CONCEIVE.

Katherine Carmichael

12/15/22

I'VE GOT MY MIND MADE UP
TO LIVE ETERNAL WITH MY MAN
SO GET OUT OF OUR WAY
FOR WE LIVE IN OUR CONDO BY THE SAND.

MY CARMICHAEL AND I
HAVE COME A LONG WAY
THIS JOURNEY WE'RE ON
IS NOT OVER, JUST A DIFFERENT DAY.

WE'VE COME AND CONQUERED
WE'VE STAYED IN IT TO WIN IT
PLEASE LET ME SAY
AND FEEL BLESSED MINUTE BY MINUTE.

WITHOUT YOU, MY CARMICHAEL
AND OUR SWEETPEA TOO
I WOULDN'T HAVE LASTED
TO SEE US THROUGH.

MY POEMS ARE SOMEWHAT ECLECTIC
THESE WORDS COMING TO ME
SO PAY CLOSE ATTENTION
AND ALLOW YOUR SOULS TO FINALLY BE FREE.

Katherine Carmichael

12/17/22

I AM UNDER THE ROCK
HIS PROTECTION SO DEVINE
I AM UNDER THE ROCK
AND I AM SO GLAD HE IS MINE.

TO KNOW, KNOW, KINOW HIM
IS TO LOVE AND WORSHIP ONLY HIM
AND I DO, YES I DO … YES I DO.

THE DAYS COME AND GO SO FAST
EVERY DAY IN ETERNITY
THEY ARE MEANT TO LAST
RESTORATION IN OUR FAMILY[S]

TO SAY WE ARE BLESSED
PUTS OUR SPIRITS TO THE TEST
THE SONG OF SOLOMON
SAYS IT'S OK THAT HE'S YOUR FINAL BEST.

THE COLORS OF THE RAINBOW
ARE A SIGNIFICANCE TO COME
I'LL HOLD MY POSITION
AND HIT THE GROUND RUNNING - SO MUCH FUN.

Katherine Carmichael

10/27/22

ONE FINAL THOUGHT OF OUR
PRECIOUS SWEETPEA...
SHE IS QUITE THE DOG.
BUT, I AM THANKFUL
THAT SHE'S NOT GOG OF MAGOG.

THE ANCIENT OF DAYS
SITS DOWN FROM UP HIGH
TO BE WITH US
AND SOON WE WILL FLY.

WE'LL FLY AWAY OLD GLORY
WE'LL FLY AWAY ...
AND WHEN WE FLY HALLELUJAH BYE & BYE
WE'LL BE GONE UP HIGH.

CPSIA information can be obtained
at www.ICGtesting.com
Printed in the USA
LVHW091024130723
751663LV00002B/85